"As you go forward into your life,
You will come upon a great chasm.
Jump.
It is not as wide as you think."

Zuni

For Dr. Jimmy "Mole Rat" Nocon,
who pours himself like water.
C.R.

This edition published in 2002.
Copyright © 1996 by The Rourke Corporation, Inc.
Text copyright © 1996 by Gloria Dominic.
Illustrations copyright © 1996 by Charles Reasoner.

Published by Troll Communications L.L.C.

Published by arrangement with The Rourke Corporation, Inc.

First paperback edition published 1998.

Printed in the United States of America.

10 9 8 7 6 5

Library of Congress Cataloging-in-Publication Data

Dominic, Gloria, 1950-
    Sunflower's Promise: a Zuni Legend/by Gloria Dominic; illustrated by Charles Reasoner.
    p. cm.—(Native American Lore and Legends)
    Includes bibliographical references.
    Summary: The clever, beautiful maiden Sunflower promises to marry the man who can rid her fields of the wild animals that are eating the beans and corn.
    ISBN 0-86593-430-4 (lib. bdg.)   ISBN 0-8167-4515-3 (pbk.)
    1. Zuni Indians—Folklore.   2. Zuni Indians—Social life and customs—Juvenile literature. [1. Zuni Indians—Folklore. 2. Zuni Indians—Social life and customs. 3. Indians of North America—New Mexico—Folklore.   4. Indians of North America—New Mexico—Social life and customs.]
I. Reasoner, Charles, ill. II. Title. III. Series.
E99.Z9D65   1996
398.2'089970789—dc20

96-9039
CIP
AC

Designed by Susan and Dave Albers

SUNFLOWER'S PROMISE

PROMISE

A ZUNI LEGEND

ADAPTED AND RETOLD BY GLORIA DOMINIC

ILLUSTRATED BY CHARLES REASONER

Troll

In a time long ago, there lived a beautiful young woman named Sunflower. Many people admired her. For not only was Sunflower beautiful, she was also rich and clever. The girl's family was one of the most prosperous among their people. So Sunflower had everything she could wish for—beautifully woven robes, exquisite moccasins, and countless pieces of the finest jewelry, made of silver and turquoise.

Sunflower lived very happily with her family. Her parents loved her deeply, and she loved them. Along with her sisters and brothers, Sunflower laughed and sang, content in the warmth of her family's devotion.

But abundance often brings its own problems, and this was true for Sunflower.

Sunflower did not see why she needed a husband. She was already quite happy. But the young men of the village did not agree with her. They would not leave Sunflower alone, so her otherwise peaceful life was continually being disturbed.

"You are the loveliest maiden of all," said one young man. "Because I cherish your beauty, I wish to be your suitor."

Sunflower refused him.

"You are rich, and so am I," said another young man. "Together think of the riches we will have."

Sunflower was not impressed.

Day after day, the unmarried men flocked around the lovely girl until she felt she could not breathe. But Sunflower was not only rich and beautiful, she was clever as well. She decided to fix this unhappy situation.

"I must think of a way to be rid of these nuisances," Sunflower said, as she walked among her many fields. Looking down, she could **not help but notice how the wild** animals had been eating all her beans and corn. She thought hard and came up with a plan. "Perhaps I can solve two problems with one solution," she said to herself with a smile.

The next morning, Sunflower announced, "I promise to marry the man who can rid my fields of the animals that are ruining them!"

Before long, news of Sunflower's announcement had spread throughout the village. One by one, the young men arrived. Each one was eager to prove his worthiness by conquering the pests of the fields.

One by one, the men failed. One young man tried to chase the animals. But when he chased them from one field, they simply ran to another. Finally the man quit, exhausted. Another suitor waited for the sun to go down, hoping to catch the pests. But at night, under the cover of darkness, the animals could not be seen, and the man thrashed aimlessly through the thick cornfields.

Others tried, but none were successful. Sunflower was not surprised. She knew that a man would need to be clever to solve such a problem, and cleverness was a rare thing.

It happened that word of Sunflower's promise reached the rather large ears of a man who lived far away. His name was Little Mole, and he was as plain as one of those creatures. Unfortunately, the women of the village thought so, too. To make matters worse, Little Mole was also very poor.

Little Mole knew that he was not very handsome. But this did not stop him from dreaming of Sunflower and thinking of the promise she had made. He had heard many wonderful things about this young woman. So he decided to go and see for himself if they were true.

Little Mole made the long journey to Sunflower's home. He humbly presented himself to her family and asked if he might meet Sunflower. The young woman's father called for her.

When she arrived, Little Mole saw that all he had heard about the girl was true. "I know I am not handsome or rich," Little Mole told her. "Yet I would like a chance to rid your fields of the animals that are eating them."

As he spoke, Sunflower noticed how brightly the young man's eyes sparkled. She noticed the sweetness of his smile. "Yes," she answered kindly, "you may try."

Sunflower repeated the terms of her bargain. "Do you still wish to try?" she asked the young man.

"I will do my best," answered Little Mole. "Although what you ask will not be an easy thing to accomplish."

Sunflower smiled. "It is for that very reason that I wish you to do it."

Again Little Mole's eyes twinkled brightly. He said good night to Sunflower and to her family. Then off he went, smiling to himself, to make his plans.

The next day, Little Mole went to Sunflower's fields. He carried a sharp hoe that he had made from a buffalo's shoulder bone and a strong stick. Shading his eyes against the hot sun, Little Mole gazed over the fields stretching out as far as he could see. "This will be hard work," he thought. Then he remembered the lovely Sunflower, took a deep breath, and pushed up his sleeves.

Little Mole got busy digging a deep trench all along the border of the field. All day he dug under the hot sun. It was an enormous task, but at last it was done. Then he lined the bottom of the trench with the most tender beans, tomatoes and squashes. He gathered the sweetest corn and laid that in the deep trench as well.

Next Little Mole set off for a small forest in the foothills of the nearby mountains. When he reached the forest, he searched among the fallen trees for branches and strong, straight tree trunks.

When he had all that he needed, he dragged the tree limbs back to the hole he had dug. With great skill, he placed the branches and poles across the trench, then covered them with chunks of sod. Upon that he set rows of cornstalks, until the hole was invisible. Last, but not least, Little Mole cooked some tasty morsels of meat and set them out among the cornstalks that covered the hole.

Tired from his hard work, Little Mole found a quiet place to take a nap and wait.

When he awoke, it was night, and the full moon was rising over the fields. Little Mole knew he was not alone. Listening closely with his rather large ears, he heard the scampering and scurrying of the night creatures as they came out to eat their fill of tender beans and sweet corn. Smiling to himself, he went back to sleep and dreamt of the beautiful Sunflower.

In the moonlight, Badger, Rat, Mouse, Mole, and Bear were all searching for their nightly feast. The quickest among them was Coyote. He smelled something extra-tempting this evening, and he ran ahead of the others to investigate.

Sniff-sniff. Coyote knew he was close now. The delicious smell of meat was near. He followed his nose, without a thought to the ground beneath him. Crash! Coyote fell into the trap.

"Yowwwl!" he cried in surprise. "What is this?" He saw he was at the bottom of a deep hole. "I'll worry about that later," Coyote told himself. Without further delay, he ate the meat that had fallen into the trap with him.

When he had finished his meal, Coyote looked up at the edge of the trench. It looked far away, but he began jumping up, again and again, trying to escape. It was not long before Coyote realized he was trapped. He threw back his head and let out a mournful howl.

Badger happened to be close by, and he put his head over the edge of the hole to see what was going on. "What is the matter?" Badger asked. "I have never heard such a sad cry!"

Coyote thought fast. "Sad?" he called to Badger. "How wrong you are! Why, I am the luckiest animal ever born. It's too bad for you that you didn't get here first."

"What do you mean?" asked Badger.

"Why, simply that the sweetest corn and most tender beans are to be found down here—and they're all mine."

Indeed, Badger could smell the food. He began to wonder if Coyote was right. He leaned a bit farther over the edge to get a better look. Then he leaned a bit more. Crash! Now he, too, was at the bottom of the trap.

Coyote let out a yowl of laughter. "Join me in my feast," he joked.

Badger was not amused. He snarled and was about to attack Coyote. Just then Coyote had an idea.

He told Badger what they must do. Soon the two creatures were singing merry songs. Their loud laughter rang out across the fields.

Curious, the other creatures drew near. Mice, rats, snakes, moles, and every other night animal gathered along the edge of the hole.

"What is happening down there?" asked Rat.

"What is that smell?" sniffed Rabbit.

"Oh, never mind," answered Badger.

"We got here first," added Coyote. "There's certainly not enough for you."

"Enough of what?" asked Mouse.

"Should we tell them?" asked Badger.

"If we must," said Coyote. "Down here we have found a more delicious feast than any of you could imagine! Never have I tasted such tender morsels."

"Are you sure there's not enough for us?" said Snake.

"Oh, come on," said Badger to Coyote, "let's share with them."

"All right," agreed Coyote. "Join us!"

Eagerly the creatures leaped, hopped, and dropped into the hole, only to find not a speck of the feast they expected. "Where is all the food?" asked Snake.

Coyote laughed. "In my stomach," he replied. Then he scampered over the backs of the animals and leaped out of the trench, laughing all the while.

"Wait for me!" cried Badger.

"No time for that now," called Coyote, and away he ran.

Down in the hole, the animals began to complain and argue.

"This was your idea."

"No, it wasn't."

"It's all your fault!"

"No, it's his fault!"

Before long, a terrible fight had begun. Such frightful yapping, snapping, biting, and clawing has not been seen or heard since that night. In the end, not one of the corn-eating, tomato-munching, bean-biting pests survived... except Coyote!

By the time the silence and the dust settled over the fields, the sun was rising in the sky. Little Mole awoke and set off to see if any creatures had fallen into his trap. Leaning over the trench, Little Mole saw what was left of the animals.

"I see you will not be eating any more beans or corn," said the young man. He noticed that all the animals were there except for one. "Where is Coyote?" he wondered. "Well, I suppose one pest is much easier to discourage than a great many."

Little Mole gathered dirt and sticks and filled up the hole. When he was finished he returned to the village to tell Sunflower that her fields were now safe.

Sunflower was very happy at the news. Her shining eyes eagerly met Little Mole's.

"I cannot lie to you," said Little Mole. "I do not know why, but Coyote was not in that hole."

"Do not worry about that," said Sunflower, smiling. She knew that a husband as clever as Little Mole was rare indeed.

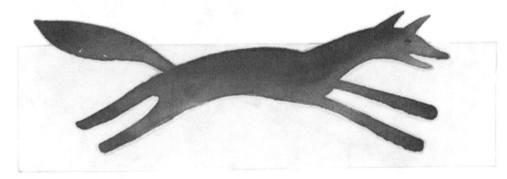

True to her word, Sunflower became the homely man's wife. The two were very happy together for the rest of their days, finding much to like about each other. In time, they had many children. They were all quite beautiful, with their father's sparkling eyes.

Through the years, word of the happy couple spread among the people. Perhaps that is why, to this day, young maidens prefer a clever man to a handsome one.

As for Coyote, he is still laughing each time he steals into the fields for his evening meal.

The Zuni

UTAH

COLORADO

ARIZONA

ZUNI

NEW MEXICO

MEXICO

TEXAS

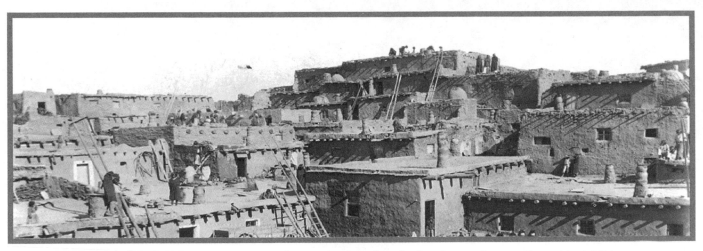

Top. This is a typical Zuni pueblo dwelling. This is a detail of a photo taken on June 19, 1897.

THE ZUNI

Zuni Homeland

They called their home "The Middle Place." For centuries, it has been near the Rio Grande River in New Mexico, close to the border of Arizona. This beautiful land is full of contrasts. Steep mesas rise dramatically out of the flat desert floor. Summer days are hot and dry, sometimes with flooding rains. Winter days bring snow and freezing cold. Along with their neighbors, the Acoma, the Hopi and others, they are collectively known as the Pueblos. Pueblo, a Spanish word that means "village" or "town," also refers to the apartment-like structure they lived in.

They were the first people the Spanish conquistadors encountered while searching for the mythical Seven Cities of Cibola. After the Spanish re-invaded in 1692, the Zunis fled to a location on top of a high, inaccessible mesa where they still live today.

They lived in multi-leveled, apartment-like structures made of logs and stone. Rectangular flat-roofed terraced rooms surrounded a central courtyard and housed many families. These dwellings had kivas (rooms for religious ceremonies), hallways and lots of ladders for getting from one level to the next.

Zuni People

They called themselves "Siwi" which meant "The people." They were desert farmers, with both men and women cultivating different crops out of the dry land by special watering techniques. The men hunted antelopes and deer. They also hunted rabbits by throwing boomerang-shaped sticks at them. Men protected the pueblo, made tools, utensils and jewelry. The women gathered and prepared the food, in addition to growing their own crops in "waffle gardens." These were gardens in rectangular compartments with little mud walls to help hold water. They also cared for the children and the homes and made pottery and baskets. Both sexes shared the work of building and repairing their home. Children were welcomed. The entire village would help him or her to grow into a responsible Zuni.

Like other Native American societies, women played an important role. They owned property and when a man married, he moved into his wife's (or mother-in-law's) home. Families related on the mother's side lived in the same house and could usually trace their descent to one female ancestor. These groups of related people were called clans. This type of kinship is called matrilineal.

Top. November 1897. Shalako dancers preparing to dance. This is a detail of the photo.

Right. A Zuni potter painting a traditional pattern on her pottery.

The Zunis were very religious and had one of the most complex native religions with very specific rituals and ceremonies. It stressed spiritual unity and the interconnection of all life in the universe.

Food and Clothing

The Zunis ate many different types of food. Meat came from deer, mountain sheep, rabbits, ducks and turkeys. Plants like berries, wild rice, nuts and cacti added to the meals and were used as medicines when appropriate. But they mostly relied on their crops for food. They grew corn, melons, herbs, chilies and onions. Corn was present at every meal in some form. Women had the time-consuming responsibility of grinding corn into meal and flour. Most women had many metates (grinding stones) for different varieties of coarseness.

Unlike other native peoples, the Pueblos were able to spin, weave and dye cotton and wool from very early on. Men wore shirts, loincloths or pants, and skin leggings. Women wore mantas—simple cotton dresses tied over one shoulder and belted at the waist. Early Zunis wore woven footwear, but later ones switched to skin moccasins. On special occasions, women wore moccasins and leg wraps made from whitened buckskin.

Top. Zuni waffle gardens in 1911.

Right. A Zuni woman doing the Yellow Basket Dance at the Inter-Tribal Indian Ceremonial in Gallup, New Mexico. This is a detail of the photo.

Below. A Zuni woman baking bread traditionally in a horno at the San Ildefonso Pueblo in 1935. This is a detail of the photo.

Zunis Today

Today, Zuni people live in cities and towns with non-natives, and on the reservation. Due to land grants in the 1680s and many treaties, the Zunis are one of the few Native nations that were not forcibly moved from their territory with the encroachment of white settlers.

Like other nations, the Zunis are experiencing an explosion of interest in the traditional ways. Many work recreating traditional crafts and arts such as making pottery and fetishes. But Zuni men and women are especially known for making highly intricate jewelry, using turquoise, coral and other semi-precious stones. Others have followed non-native careers such as medicine, law, writing, and fire fighting.

Top. A Zuni owl fetish made from the mineral malachite.

Bottom. A collection of beautifully decorated Zuni clay pottery in 1925. This is a detail of the photo.

Della Casi, a Zuni jeweler.

Glossary

Cibola: A mythical land filled with gold and riches

Fetish: A representative image of a god decorated with paint and feathers. Known to be both a work of art and a symbol of great religious significance

Kiva: A special room for religious ceremonies, usually entered by a ladder through the ceiling

Kachina: Spirit being who enters the bodies of selected men wearing masks and performing sacred dances

Matrilineal: Tracing descent through the female line

Mesa: A mountain that stands alone from other mountains, usually with a flat top. Comes from the Spanish word for "table"

Metate: Grinding stone

Top. Zuni Dick, a jeweler using a pump drill at Zuni Pueblo.

Bottom. A winged owl Zuni fetish with turquoise eyes. The magical powers of owls played a prominent role in many Zuni legends.

Pueblo: Groups originating in Central America, now in the American Southwest. Also means the communal dwelling the people live in. Comes from the Spanish word for "village" or "town"

Pekwin: The head of Zuni village government

Waffle garden: Garden with rectangular compartments enclosed by ridges of clay or earth to retain water

Above. A Zuni kachina maker at Zuni Pueblo around 1915.

Important Dates

1492: Columbus lands in the Americas

1680: Pueblo Revolt drives the Spanish out of the area for twelve years

1692: The Spanish re-invade the area, causing the Zunis to flee to the top of a high, inaccessible mesa, the site of their present home

1848: The Treaty of Guadalupe Hidalgo grants the U.S. possession of the present-day states of New Mexico and Arizona

1872: Navaho teach silversmithing to the Zunis

Top. A Zuni coyote fetish.

Left. A kachina mask.

Above. March 23, 1882, Frank Cushing and a group of Zuni Pueblo Indians taken to Boston, Massachusetts, to conduct ceremonies and replenish their supply of sacred sea water.

1924: All Native Americans born in the U.S. declared citizens

1968: Indian Civil Rights Act gives Native Americans the right to govern themselves on their reservations

1969: Zuni Comprehensive Development Plan creates jobs and improves education and living conditions

PHOTO CREDITS

We want to extend a special thank you to Arthur L. Olivas, from the Palace of the Governors, a Division of the Museum of New Mexico, Santa Fe, New Mexico, for all of his help in acquiring images for this book.

Pages 32-33: Cliffs, Photo by Dave Albers
Shiwawatiwa, Photo by Edward S. Curtis. Courtesy Museum of New Mexico, #143734
Pages 34-35: Map, Illustration by Dave Albers.
Zuni Pueblo, Photo by Ben Wittick. Courtesy Museum of New Mexico, #56120
Pages 36-37: Dancers, Photo by Ben Wittick. Courtesy Museum of New Mexico, #16443
Potter, Photo by Merl LaVoy. Courtesy Museum of New Mexico, #151917
Pages 38-39: Waffle Gardens, Photo by Jesse L. Nusbaum, #8742, and Zuni Dancer, Photo by Mullarky, #30956;
Baking Bread, Photo by T. Harmon Parkhurst, #20416. All three images Courtesy Museum of New Mexico
Pages 40-41: Fetish, Photo by Dave Albers, Courtesy of a Private Collection
Pottery, Photo by Edward S. Curtis. Courtesy Museum of New Mexico, #144672
Jeweler, Photo by Frasher. Courtesy Museum of New Mexico, #9189
Pages 42-43: Zuni Dick, Photo by J.R. Willis. Courtesy Museum of New Mexico, #108581
Fetish, Photo by Dave Albers. Courtesy of a Private Collection
Kachina maker, Courtesy Museum of New Mexico, #68770
Pages 44-45: Fetish, Courtesy of a Private Collection. Mask, Dover Books
Group of Zuni Leaders, Photo by James W. Black, Courtesy Museum of New Mexico, #9146
Pages 46-48: Zuni Pueblo, Courtesy a Private Collection
Three women, Courtesy Museum of New Mexico, #4924
Agave and roadrunner, Illustration by Dave Albers

ZUNI   BIBLIOGRAPHY

Baldwin, Gordon C. Indians of the Southwest. New York: Putnam, 1970.

Brandon, Alvin M. The American Heritage Book of Indians. New York: American Heritage Publishing Co., 1961.

Bonvillain, Nancy. The Zuni. New York: Chelsea House Publishers, 1995.

Crampton, C. Gregory. The Zunis of Cibola. Salt Lake City, UT: University of Utah Press, 1977.

Erdoes, Richard. The Pueblo Indians. New York: Funk & Wagnalls, 1967.

Erdoes, Richard. The Rain Dance People: The Pueblo Indians, Their Past and Present. New York: Knopf, 1976.

Leighton, Dorothea C. and John Adair. People of the Middle Place. New Haven, CT: Human Relations Area Files Press, 1966.

Ortiz, Alfonso. The Pueblo. New York: Chelsea House Publishers, 1994.

Sando, Joe S. The Pueblo Indians. San Francisco: The Indian Historian Press, 1976.

Sturtevant, William C., General Editor. Handbook of North American Indians, Southwest (Volume 9). Washington: Smithsonian Institution, 1979.

Waldman, Carl. Encyclopedia of North American Tribes. New York: Facts on File, 1988.

Wolfson, Evelyn. From Abenaki to Zuni: A Dictionary of Native American Tribes. New York: Walker, 1988.

Above. Three Zuni women dressed in traditional clothing and carrying clay pots on their heads.